PLAY THE
DRUMS

HINKLER
BOOKS

CAMERON SKEWS

I would like to thank my parents John and Kay for supporting my drum habit and putting up with me tapping everything in sight, and thanks to the many teachers who inspired me to keep learning: John Gradon, Andrew Collins and Justin Humphries, to name just a few.
C.S.

Author: Cameron Skews
Editor: Louise Coulthard
Art Director: Paul Scott
Photography: Ned Meldrum and Daryl Snowdon
Prepress: Graphic Print Group

Thank you to

www.drumtek.com.au

Pearl Drums
Zildjian Cymbals
Vater Drumsticks

and Tim Nikolsky

First published in 2008
by Hinkler Books Pty Ltd
45–55 Fairchild Street
Heatherton Victoria 3202 Australia
www.hinklerbooks.com

Printed and bound in China

2 4 6 8 10 9 7 5 3
08 10 12 11 09

ISBN 978 1 7418 2877 1

CONTENTS

INTRODUCTION

This book is an introduction to the oldest instrument in the world. People have been playing drums for thousands of years and they are the most universally used instrument across all the cultures of the world.

I started playing the drums when I was 13 years old and wanted to start a band with my school friends. That first afternoon I sat in front of a drum kit was the beginning of a lifelong passion for the effect that playing a beat can have on people.

The drums are first and foremost an accompanying instrument. I love a good drum solo as much as the next person, but when you are playing drums, 99 percent of the time you are accompanying other people. As a drummer, most of your time is spent laying down a solid groove, over which vocals or instrumental soloists complete the picture that any great piece of music creates.

The aim of this book is to take you from the first moment you pick up a pair of drumsticks to being able to play through an entire song. You will learn how to develop good technique in your hands and your feet; the basics of how to read music; how to play a rock beat; how beats are applied to a song; and how to tie those beats together using fills.

Good luck, and let's get started!

THE DRUM KIT

There are two types of percussion instruments that make up a drum kit: drums and cymbals.

DRUMS

It is very important to understand how a drum works, particularly if you want to get the best sound out of your drum kit. A drum is made up of the following parts:

THE SHELL

The size of the drum shell and the type of material it is made out of have the biggest impact on the tone or sound of a drum. Hitting the drum skin makes a sound, which vibrates and is amplified in the shell. Drum shells are made out of metals such as steel, aluminium, brass, bronze and gold, and woods like maple, birch or mahogany.

THE DRUM HEADS OR SKINS

A drum has one head on the top and another on the bottom. Drum heads are fastened tightly around the shell of the drum, so that when you hit them, they create a vibration. This vibration is where the sound of the drum originates from. Drum heads used to be made of animal skins, which is why they are also referred to as 'skins'. These days, they are made from plastic and come in a variety of styles, depending on the type of sound you want and the sort of music you play.

THE RIMS AND LUGS

The rims are metal rings that hold the drum heads on to the shells. Lugs are screws that attach the rims (and therefore the heads) to the shell and allow you to tighten or loosen the heads, which tunes the drums.

shell

lugs

drum head/skin

rims

CYMBALS

Cymbals are the other major component of a drum kit.

Cymbals are thin round disks made of various types of metals, including bronze, brass and silver. Cymbals create different types of bright, shimmering sounds when they are struck.

A cymbal consists of the bell and the body. Each part of the cymbal creates a different and distinctive sound.

bell

body

cymbal

THE PARTS OF A DRUM KIT

A standard drum kit is made up of the following drums and cymbals:

BASS DRUM

This is the largest and deepest drum in the kit. It is played with the foot, using a foot pedal, which is why it is also called a 'kick drum'.

TOMS

There are three toms on a standard drum kit. The toms can be mounted on the bass drum (known as mounted toms) or on a stand or rack (known as rack toms). They may also sit on the floor on legs, in which case they are called a floor tom.

bass drum

Mounted toms on the bass drum

floor tom

SNARE DRUM

The snare drum plays a very important role in a drum kit. It differs from other drums because it has a group of curled wires, called snares, stretched across the bottom head. The snares are held in place by a switch or a lever on the side of the shell. When the switch is on, the vibration from the skins is absorbed by the snares, producing a sharp crack. The snare can also be turned off so the wires are not touching the skin, and then the sound produced is similar to other drums.

snare switch

snares

snare drum

HI-HAT

The hi-hat is made up of two cymbals, a stand and a foot pedal. The two cymbals are held together or apart by the foot pedal at the base of the stand. Hi-hats make different sounds depending on whether they are closed tightly together, loosely touching or completely apart.

CRASH CYMBAL

Crash cymbals come in different sizes and are used to make a loud, attention-grabbing 'crash'. They are often used to signify changes or accents in the music. Different types of crash cymbals have a shorter or longer 'decay', which is the length of time it takes for the cymbal's sound to stop. Generally, the bigger the crash, the longer the decay.

hi-hat

crash cymbal

RIDE CYMBAL

The ride cymbal is the largest and heaviest of the cymbals. It is played with a constant rhythm or pattern, to 'ride' the music. Unlike the crash cymbal, the ride has a very short decay, allowing you to play a quick succession of notes that are clear and don't wash into each other.

HARDWARE

In addition to the drums and cymbals, the drum kit consists of hardware, which holds all the parts together. Drum hardware includes cymbal stands, the hi-hat stand, the bass drum pedal and tom mounts.

BASS DRUM PEDAL

The bass drum pedal is made up of a footboard, a mount and a beater. The footboard is attached to the beater, and both are held in position by a spring. When the footboard is pushed down, the beater is pulled towards the drum. The spring can be tightened or loosened, based on how much resistance you want against your foot.

HI-HAT STAND

The hi-hat stand sits next to the snare drum. It consists of a stand with a pedal that pulls down on a rod inside the stand's shaft. Pressing the footboard makes the rod move up and down. The top cymbal is attached to the rod with a hi-hat clutch, which grips the cymbal and the rod, binding them together. The top cymbal moves up and down to open or close the hi-hat when the pedal is pressed.

CYMBAL STANDS AND BOOM STAND

Cymbal stands hold the cymbals in position around the drum kit. Boom stands have an adjustable arm, so the cymbals can be placed in more positions around the drum kit. The boom stand is counterbalanced so the cymbal can be suspended over the kit.

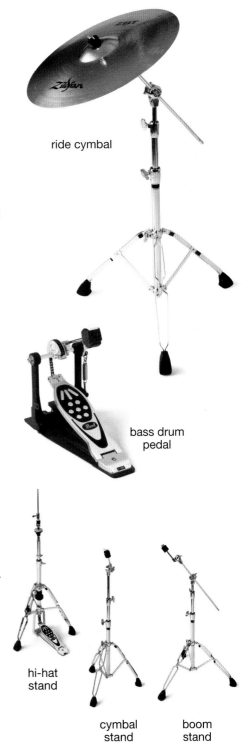

ride cymbal

bass drum pedal

hi-hat stand

cymbal stand

boom stand

SETTING UP THE KIT

There is no correct way to set up a drum kit. Everyone sets up in a different way, depending on how they like to play, but there are a couple of things that are worth remembering to make sure that you get the most out of your kit.

When setting up, the main thing to consider is how you move. You should be focusing as much energy as possible on playing the drums, not on trying to get from one drum to another. Think about the most natural path that your arms take to move around the kit and use that as a guide for how you set up the drums. It is essential that you can reach everything with ease. It might look good to have all the cymbals sitting flat on their stands or the drums placed really high, but if it makes them difficult to play properly, it probably isn't worth it. The less energy you need to use to reach everything, the more you can put into your playing.

Nearly everything on the drums is held in position by a screw – for example, the legs on the floor tom, the position and height of the cymbals and the angle of the toms. Always make sure that everything is secured tightly, but don't overdo it; screwing in any part of your kit too tightly can cause damage and reduce the life of your equipment.

When you set up your cymbal and snare stands, make sure that the stand legs are wide enough to stop the whole thing from toppling over, but not so wide that it is difficult to position the stand close to the kit. The width of the object they are holding is a good indication of how wide the stand's legs should be. There is no need to open the legs down as far as they go; slightly wider than the width of the cymbal or snare is enough.

 X  X  ✓ The correct width of the stand legs

What You Need to Get Started

Drumsticks

If you visit a music store, you will see hundreds of different types of drumsticks. There are endless combinations of size, length, weight and style, but amongst all of those sticks is one that is perfect for you.

A drumstick consists of the following parts:

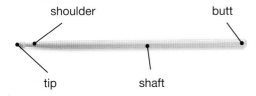

When choosing a stick, consider the size of your hands before thinking about the style of music you like to play. You should be able to easily hold the stick in your hand and control it with your fingers. If the stick is too long or heavy, it will be unmanageable and will hinder your playing; if it is too light or thin, it won't feel solid in your hands.

Try a few different sizes of stick to see which suits you best. The standard drumstick sizes, from lightest to heaviest, are 7A, 5A, 5B and 2B. Remember, don't select a stick that is too big for your hands, as it will make things difficult as you progress.

Another decision when selecting drumsticks is choosing the tip. The tip does most of the playing, so it is very important.

There are two types of tips: wood and nylon. Wood tips give a natural, warm sound, while nylon tips have a harder, brighter sound. It is best to use nylon tips when you start learning, as they last longer than wood, which can chip and will need to be replaced.

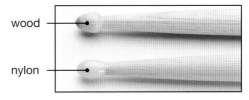

When selecting sticks, play them on a practice pad in the store to make sure they feel balanced and comfortable. Check there are no unusual patterns or dark spots in the wood as this can indicate flaws and weaknesses in the wood. To check that a stick is straight, roll it across a flat surface; if it is bent, the tips will move up and down.

The last thing to consider when choosing sticks is the type of music you play. Loud music that the drums need to cut through calls for heavier sticks; quieter music is better suited to lighter ones.

METRONOME

A metronome helps to mark time and play at a constant speed. This is a really important thing for all drummers to learn right from the start, as other musicians in a band will often look to the drummer to keep them in time.

PRACTICE PAD

You will get the most out of practicing by playing on the drums, but sometimes that isn't an option. A practice pad has a similar feel to playing on a drum and lets you practice your technique without making too much noise.

CHOOSING A DRUM KIT

Choosing your first drum kit is really exciting! Just like choosing drumsticks, the most important thing is to get a kit that suits you and the music that you want to play.

As with all musical instruments, you get what you pay for, so spend as much as you can afford on your drums. Drum kits can be expensive, but if you look after them, they can last for years, so it is worth spending the money on a good instrument to begin with.

DRUMS

Start out with a standard five-piece drum kit (bass drum, snare and three toms). Bigger kits with racks of toms or multiple bass drums look impressive, but you end up spending money on extra drums instead of better-sounding ones. You won't need all of that equipment, especially when starting out.

When you check out a kit, make sure that nothing is loose or rattling and that all the stands and hardware are sturdy. Check the drums to make sure that the rims are straight and that the covers around the shells are fitted properly, with no bubbling.

Most importantly of all, play them! Sit at the kit and hit each drum at different volume levels to hear what differences there are in the sound; some kits sound great when played loudly but lose their quality when played softly, or vice versa. A good drum kit should sound great at all volume levels. Make sure the snare easily turns on and off and that there isn't too much buzz or rattle when it is hit.

Once you have selected your kit, ask the store to tune it for you. Learning the best way to tune your drums takes time and patience. Getting it tuned by a professional means at least you can start learning with your drums sounding their best.

CYMBALS

There are plenty of great beginner cymbal packs made by the top cymbal manufacturers. A basic beginner's cymbal set-up should comprise hi-hats, a crash and a ride. Cheap cymbals will bend, buckle or crack when played, so it is worth paying a little extra to ensure that you get sturdy cymbals which will last.

How to Hold the Sticks

Your technique, or how you hold the sticks and hit the drums, is very important. Good technique opens up endless possibilities with the drums; bad technique severely limits how creative you can be when you play.

The first step to learning how to hold the sticks is to find the correct height to hold them. The best spot for your thumb and index finger is about a third of the way up the stick. Holding the stick here means you get more energy back from the stick when it bounces on the drum. This makes the stick and the rebound energy from the drum do some of the work for you.

Find a spot about a third of the way up the stick and hook your index finger underneath at this point.

Keep supporting the stick like this and let it bounce on a practice pad.

If your hand is too far up the stick, there won't be enough weight at the front for the stick to drop naturally; too low down the stick and there will be too much weight at the front, smothering the natural bounce of the stick.

It can help to mark the sticks at the correct height with a pen.

Once you have found the best spot to hold the stick, focus on the thumb and index finger. These two digits are the most important point of the grip, called the fulcrum. The fulcrum is where the stick pivots from.

1 Grip the stick between your index finger and thumb at the balance point marked on the stick.

2 Close your other fingers around the stick so that the first joint of each finger is curled around the shaft. The butt of the stick should pass along the groove at the bottom of your palm.

3 Turn your hand around until the back is facing up.

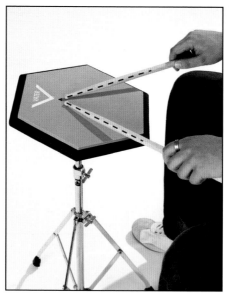

Now repeat the process for the other hand. It should resemble this image. If the sticks make an arrow shape from your hands to the tips of the stick, this is a good indication that your technique is correct.

How to Hit the Drums and Cymbals

Hitting a drum or a cymbal may seem straightforward enough, but there are a number of important things to keep in mind so you get the best sound out of your kit.

Drums

Consistency and accuracy are two of the most important skills that a good drummer needs. To create a solid beat, you must be able to maintain consistent speed, volume and sound with all four limbs at the same time.

To create a consistent sound, you must be accurate about where you hit the drum. For example, hit the snare drum as close to the middle as you can. Now hit the snare with the other hand, but aim for a spot closer to the edge of the head. Do they sound different? Different parts of the drum, such as closer to the middle or near the edge, have a different pitch.

Pitch is a musical term for a high- or low-sounding note, made, in this case, when you hit the snare. The pitch of the drum is higher closer to the rim because the head is tighter and vibrates less. In the middle of the drum, the pitch is lower because the head is free to move more. This is important, because when you play a drum, the sound should be consistent.

If you play one stroke after another on the snare drum but your right and left hands hit different parts of the drum, the sound will be inconsistent. Play with both hands in the same spot and the sound will be even. Try this with the other drums or cymbals; even a practice pad has different pitches if your strokes aren't played in the same spot.

While the ability to produce different sounds from a drum can be a great tool as you progress, it is a good idea to aim for consistency when you are beginning to learn. Always try to keep your strokes as close to the center of each drum head as possible.

CYMBALS

Cymbals offer you a huge range of sounds and you can get some really interesting effects, depending on how you approach them with your sticks. Experiment using the tip and the shoulder of your stick against different parts of the cymbal, including the bell and the edge.

Hitting cymbal on the bell

Hitting cymbal on the body

Ride and hi-hat cymbals are mostly played with the tip of the stick, so you can hear the stick clearly through the music.

Crash cymbals sound just like their name and are often played with the shoulder of the stick to get a louder sound. To get the best out of your crash, try to glance the stick off the right or left side rather than right down the middle. If you drive your stick straight down the center, you not only stop the natural vibrations of the cymbal, but you also risk breaking it.

It is important not to continue to drive the stick into the cymbal once you have hit it. Think of your stick as a whip: flick at the cymbal, pulling the stick back once you have hit it. This will also draw out the sound of the crash.

Basic Rudiments

Like ingredients for a chef or paint for an artist, rudiments are the basic elements of drumming. The better you understand and know how to use them, the better the final result. There are different types of rudiments, but focus on three basic ones to begin with: the single stroke, the double stroke and the paradiddle.

When you are practising rudiments, it is a good idea to play them in different ways: quiet and loud; fast and slow; on drums and on practice pads; hands together on one drum and apart on different ones. The more you practice them, the better everything you play on the drums will sound, but there is one very important rule to remember when you practice your rudiments: consistency.

Consistent sound

Play each stroke at the same volume and on the same spot on the drum so that each stroke sounds exactly alike, regardless of which hand is playing. Test yourself by closing your eyes and listening carefully; if you can hear a difference in the pitch or sound of the strokes, try and work out why and fix the problem. One quick and easy way to spot if your sound isn't consistent is by watching the height of your strokes. Higher strokes are louder and if one hand is playing higher strokes than the other, you won't be able to get a consistent sound.

Consistent tempo

Tempo is the speed at which you play music. It is very important for a drummer to be able to maintain a steady tempo, whether it is fast or slow. When you practice, pick a tempo and stay at that pace. If you want to play an exercise faster or slower, stop playing and start again at the new tempo. This will get you used to maintaining a solid tempo, which is a great attribute of any drummer. A metronome is a great tool to help you practice keeping a steady time.

SINGLE STROKE

The single stroke is the most fundamental rudiment. It consists of one stroke followed by another, with hands alternating. The single stroke can be played starting with your right hand or your left:

It is a good idea to change the hand that you begin each exercise with, so you don't favor your right or your left hand too much. A stopwatch or clock can be a great tool to assist you when you are practicing your rudiments. Start by aiming to play a single stroke for 30 seconds at a consistent tempo. Once you reach that target, aim for a minute without stopping. Don't progress to the next target time until you can play consistent and even strokes all the way through.

DOUBLE STROKE

As the name suggests, the double stroke consists of two strokes with one hand followed by two strokes with the other. When you play the double stroke, try to make it sound as consistent as a single stroke. Play the double stroke for 30 seconds at a consistent tempo, then aim for 1 minute before increasing the speed:

PARADIDDLE

The paradiddle is a combination of the single and double strokes. The sticking pattern for a paradiddle is:

As you can see, the first two strokes are single strokes, followed by a double stroke. This leaves you starting the second paradiddle with the other hand. It is called a paradiddle because that is the sound that it makes when you play it.

R	L	R	R	L	R	L	L
pa	ra	did	dle	pa	ra	did	dle

Practice the sticking pattern until you can play it ten times without making a mistake. Once you can confidently play a paradiddle, we can add the final element: the accent.

ACCENTS

In music, an accented note looks like this:

The accent arrow above a note indicates it should be played louder than the other notes around it, so that it stands out. The easiest way to play a stroke louder is to lift the stick a little higher on that stroke. The higher the stick is when it starts its trip to the drum, the more time it has to accelerate and the faster it will be traveling when it hits the drum.

You can test this. It doesn't matter how hard you try to hit the drum – if your stick is 2 inches from the skin, it isn't going to make a lot of noise. Now try hitting the drum with the stick starting at the height of your shoulder. It makes a big difference, doesn't it?

unaccented stroke

accented stroke

In a paradiddle, the first note of each paradiddle is accented:

	R	L	R	R	L	R	L	L

The double stroke at the end of each paradiddle gives you extra time to lift your stick higher for the accent that follows. Practice this slowly until you get the hang of playing the accent comfortably.

PRACTICING RUDIMENTS

Practicing rudiments is very important. Even if you can only spare ten minutes a day, spend that ten minutes working on your rudiments and you will see a vast improvement in your playing in as little as a couple of weeks.

If you want to spice up your rudiment practice, try coming up with a few different ways you can play rudiments around the drums.

Here are some examples to get you started:

SINGLE STROKE

Single stroke around the drum kit, with 4 strokes on each drum.

Single stroke around the drum kit, with 2 strokes on each drum.

DOUBLE STROKE

Double stroke around the drum kit, with 4 strokes on each drum.

Double stroke around the drum kit, with 2 strokes on each drum.

PARADIDDLE

Paradiddle on the snare drum, playing accents on the toms.

FOOT TECHNIQUE AND SITTING AT THE DRUMS

Which foot plays the bass drum and which plays the hi-hat can depend on whether you are right- or left-handed. Most right-handed players play the bass drum with their right foot and the hi-hat with their left foot, and vice versa for left-handed drummers.

When you sit at the drum kit, make sure that it isn't too close or too far away. If you have to reach out with your toes to touch the bass drum, most likely you aren't sitting close enough. Likewise, if your knee is touching the rim of the bass drum, you might want to sit back a bit.

Set your stool to a height where the top of your legs are flat. You may decide later that you prefer playing with the stool higher or lower than this for balance, but when you are learning, this is a pretty good place to start.

A good indication that you are the right distance from the bass drum is if you can draw a straight line from the front of your knee down to your ankle.

Bass drum

There are two ways of playing the bass drum pedal: heel-up and heel-down. Neither is incorrect and many drummers use both, depending on the situation.

Playing heel-down

Playing heel-down gives more control at different volumes and can be easier when you are first learning to play.

To play heel-down, place your heel at the base of the bass drum pedal. Let the rest of your foot lie naturally up the footboard. Pivoting from your ankle, tap the beater into the head, using the same action as tapping your foot on the ground.

Playing heel-up

Heel-up playing is often used for high-energy, loud playing, as it utilizes the natural weight of your leg to drive the beater hard into the drum head.

To play heel-up, place the ball of your foot about three quarters of the way up the footboard with your heel off the ground and let the weight of your leg push the beater into the bass drum head. This is the resting position where your leg will sit naturally between strokes. With your heel still off the ground, push off the footboard, as though you are hopping.

As your leg lifts up, the footboard will also spring up. Try to maintain contact with the footboard between when your leg goes up and when it comes back down again. This is important, because if your foot completely leaves the pedal, you may lose control of it, which can be disastrous. When your leg comes back down, allow your foot to act as a spring, as though you are landing but preparing to jump again.

HI-HAT PEDAL

Just as both hands use the same technique for holding drumsticks, the principles that apply to the bass drum foot also apply to the hi-hat pedal. The hi-hat pedal is used to control whether the hi-hats are open or closed. This varies the type of sounds the hi-hat can create, ranging from a 'sizzling' sound when open to a tight 'chick' when closed.

To begin, keep the hi-hat closed. Rest the weight of your leg on the hi-hat footboard so you get a clear 'chick' sound when you hit the hi-hat with the tip of your stick. This can be done with the heel up or down, depending on what feels most comfortable for you.

Playing the hi-hat heel up

Playing the hi-hat heel down

HOW TO READ MUSIC

Now that you have learned some basic sticking patterns, it is a good time to learn how to read music. Reading music can seem difficult at first, but if you keep a couple of basic things in mind, it can be easier than reading words. It will also allow you to continue learning new things on the drums without relying on someone to show you how.

THE STAFF

The five lines shown below make up the musical staff. The staff is where the notes are hung. Where they sit on or in between these lines will determine what drum or cymbal you hit.

DRUMS

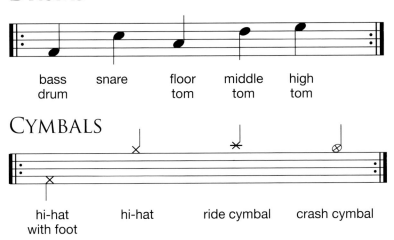

CYMBALS

A BAR

Music is broken up into bars (or measures), which are indicated by a bar line.

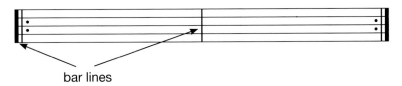

NOTES AND RESTS

There are two main types of characters in music: notes and rests.

NOTES

In written music, notes tell you when and what to play. For piano, that means which keys you press; for drums, it means which drums or cymbals you hit.

Notes are made up of a head, a stem and a tail.

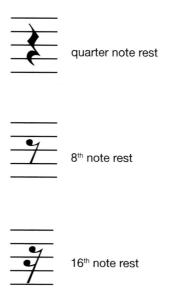

stem — tail — head

There are many different types of notes but to begin with, let's look at three of them.

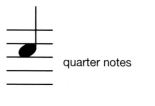

quarter notes

8th notes

16th notes

You can recognize one type of note from another by its tail. Quarter notes have no tail, 8th notes have one tail and 16th notes have two. The type of note indicates how long or short it is played for, or in our case, how you count it. When a note appears in a lower part of the staff, the stem and tail hang down instead of pointing up.

RESTS

Rests are the opposite of notes. As the name suggests, rests tell you when to 'rest' or to not play. Rests are important because in music, the space between notes is as important as the notes themselves. For every note, there is an equivalent rest which takes up the same space in the bar.

quarter note rest

8th note rest

16th note rest

The size of a bar, which determines how many notes or rests can fit in it, is determined by the time signature.

TIME SIGNATURES

The time signature determines how many notes fit in a bar and what value of note makes up one beat. Most modern music is in 4/4 time, which is also called common time.

The top 4 indicates that there are 4 beats in the bar, so you count '1 2 3 4'.

The bottom 4 indicates that the beat is on the quarter notes.

COUNTING NOTES

The most important thing to help you read music and understand note and rest values is counting. There are different ways of counting each type of note so that you will always know how to play quarter, 8th or 16th notes. This is an easy way to learn to read music quickly, but it relies on you counting what you are playing out loud. Sometimes this can feel a little silly, but you will learn more quickly by saying the numbers while you are playing, as it focuses you on the task more.

QUARTER NOTES

In 4/4 time, the beat is made up of quarter notes. There are four in a bar, so you count quarter notes:

It is as simple as that. When you hear a band starting a song and someone counts off '1 2 3 4', they are counting one bar of quarter notes out loud so everyone in the band knows:

- the speed of the song (you will never hear someone count '1 2 3 4' really fast and then hear a slow song start up); and
- when to start (the song starts when they reach '1' again, straight after 4).

Remember to count out loud while you are playing.

QUARTER NOTE EXERCISES

Try playing single stroke for a bar of quarter notes. It looks like this:

Now try playing four bars of single strokes as quarter notes without stopping:

Try the same exercise with double stroke and paradiddles.

A bar of double stroke:

Four bars of double stroke:

Two bars of paradiddle:

Four bars of paradiddle:

Counting can be difficult at first, but once you get the hang of it, you will find that your playing is more consistent and your timing is rock solid.

8ᵀᴴ Notes

Now that you have learned counting, applying it to different note values is a lot easier. As you can probably guess from the name, there are eight 8th notes in a bar. Count 8th notes like this:

As you can see, you still have quarter notes in there on 1, 2, 3 and 4, but now there are also the 'and' notes in between, making up eight notes in the bar.

8ᵀᴴ Note Exercises

Count a bar of quarter notes and then a bar of 8th notes. Remember that the time between 1, 2, 3, 4 should be the same across both bars, but in the second bar, count 'and' between each of the numbers (i.e. the 8th notes will be twice as fast).

Now try playing your rudiments as 8th notes. The double stroke is particularly suited to 8th notes, as 1, 2, 3 and 4 all correspond to each change of hands.

1	+	2	+	3	+	4	+
R	R	L	L	R	R	L	L

Don't forget to count out loud!

Four bars of single stroke as 8th notes:

Four bars of double stroke as 8th notes:

Four bars of paradiddle as 8th notes:

16TH NOTES

By now, you will have guessed that there are sixteen 16th notes in a bar; that is, two 16th notes for every 8th note and four for every quarter note. You count 16th notes like this:

You can see there are still quarter notes (1, 2, 3, 4) and 8th notes (1 + 2 + 3 + 4 +), but in between there are 'e' and 'a', making up 16th notes.

16TH NOTE EXERCISES

Try playing your rudiments while counting 16th notes. The paradiddle is particularly suited to 16th notes as the accent will fall on 1, 2, 3 and 4 along with the beat.

```
1   e   +   a   2   e   +   a   3   e   +   a   4   e   +   a
R   L   R   R   L   R   L   L   R   L   R   R   L   R   L   L
```

Two bars of single stroke:

Two bars of double stroke:

Two bars of paradiddle:

THE ROCK BEAT

Now that you have learned the hand and foot techniques, the basic rudiments and how to recognize and count the different notes, it is time to pull all of that knowledge together and learn a basic rock beat.

There are three parts of the kit that go together to make a basic rock beat:

- Hi-hat
- Snare
- Bass drum.

Start by looking at each part individually, then pair the parts up in different combinations and finally put them all together.

THE HI-HAT

The hi-hat is the glue that holds the beat together. It provides a steady pattern that keeps the time going against the louder, sometimes-changing bass drum and snare. Most drummers play the hi-hat with their leading hand (right if right-handed, left if left-handed), but there is no right or wrong way, so use whichever hand is most comfortable.

The hi-hat part looks like this:

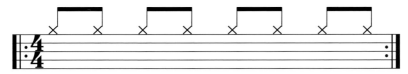

Recognize these notes? They are 8th notes, so you play them 1 + 2 + 3 + 4 +. With your foot holding the hi-hat closed, try playing this 8th note pattern on top of the hi-hat, while counting out loud:

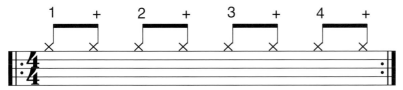

As with the rudiments, practice this pattern at different tempos and volumes until you can play it comfortably.

THE SNARE DRUM

The snare drum is the driving force behind a rock beat. It creates a pulse that pushes the music forward.

The snare is played on 2 and on 4 with your other hand: that is, the hand that isn't playing the hi-hat. The snare part looks like this:

While counting 8th notes out loud, try playing the snare pattern.

THE BASS DRUM

The bass drum pattern plays against the snare, complementing it to fill out the beat.

The bass drum is played on 1 and on 3 and looks like this:

While counting 8th notes out loud, try playing the bass drum pattern.

COMBINING THE ELEMENTS

Now that you understand the elements of the rock beat individually, let's put them together in pairs. For all of these exercises, remember to play the hi-hat and snare with the correct hand and not swap it with the hand you will be using when all of the elements are combined.

Here are the snare and the bass drum together. Try playing this pattern, remembering to count 8th notes aloud at the same time.

Now try combining the hi-hat pattern with the snare pattern. On 2 and 4, both your hands will come down together, one on the snare and one on the hi-hat. Make sure you start slowly, and count all of the 8th notes aloud.

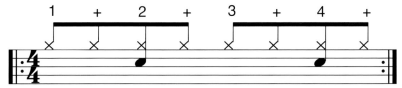

Don't rush any of these exercises. Make sure that you are comfortable before you move to the next one.

Once you are confident with the hi-hat and snare combination, try combining the hi-hat and bass drum, leaving out the snare. The hi-hat stays the same, but this time, the bass drum will come down with it on 1 and 3.

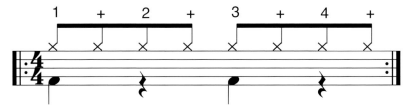

THE BASIC ROCK BEAT

Now it is time to pull all of the elements together and play your first rock beat. Try starting by playing one bar of just the hi-hat, then introduce the other elements. Remember to count and play slowly.

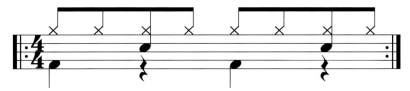

It can take a couple of tries to get it right. If you can't quite get all of the parts to match, try practicing some of the earlier combinations that only involve two limbs. Don't be discouraged! This is a lot more difficult than rubbing your stomach and patting your head, and a lot of people can't even do that!

Once you are able to play the entire beat through once, aim for two and then three times. The goal is to comfortably play the rock beat continuously, without stopping.

If you have got the hang of it, well done! This rock beat is the basis for most popular music styles and can be played with all sorts of songs. Have a listen to the radio or your favorite CDs and count along with them. You will soon begin to hear the parts of the rock beat clearly.

BASS DRUM VARIATIONS

Now that you can play a basic rock beat, you can try making it a little more interesting by introducing 8th note variations on the bass drum.

The following exercises introduce the concept of changing the bass drum pattern while maintaining the same snare and hi-hat patterns.

As always, remember to count out loud. If you are having difficulty with any of the beats, slow down and try again. The aim is to play each of these for a minute without stopping. Have fun!

Exercise 1

Exercise 2

Exercise 3

Exercise 4

Exercise 5

Exercise 6

Exercise 7

Exercise 8

Exercise 9

Exercise 10

Exercise 11

Exercise 12

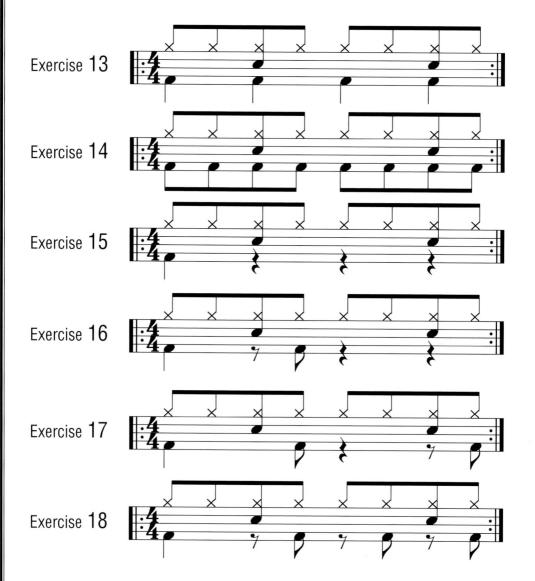

Exercise 13

Exercise 14

Exercise 15

Exercise 16

Exercise 17

Exercise 18

OFF-BEAT BASS DRUM VARIATIONS

Most of the rock beat patterns in the last section featured bass drum combinations that were 'on' the beat. You will recall that the two 4s in the time signature 4/4 indicate that there are 4 beats in the bar and that the beat is on the quarter note. Playing 'with' or 'on' the beat in a bar of 4/4 means playing notes or patterns that emphasize 1, 2, 3 and 4.

Emphasizing the 'off beat' means focusing on those notes that are not 'on the beat'. The rock beat below is an example of a beat that emphasizes the off beat. As you can see, all of the bass drum notes are on the off beat.

Exercise 1

Here are some more off-beat bass drum exercises:

Exercise 2

Exercise 3

Exercise 4

Exercise 5

Exercise 6

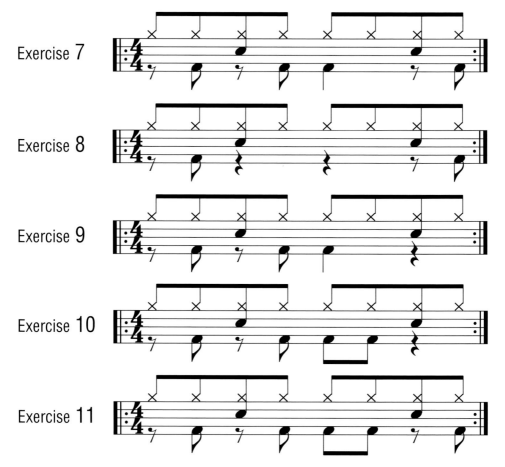

Exercise 7

Exercise 8

Exercise 9

Exercise 10

Exercise 11

SNARE AND BASS DRUM VARIATIONS

Here are some 8th note variations on the snare drum. Some of these exercises are useful beats and some are really good independence exercises that will help your playing.

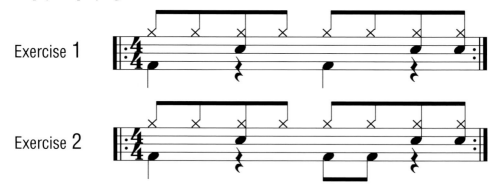

Exercise 1

Exercise 2

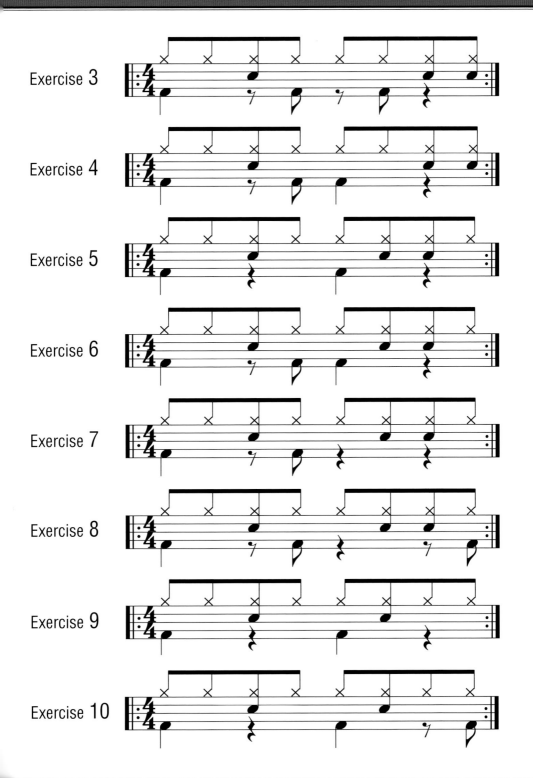

Exercise 3

Exercise 4

Exercise 5

Exercise 6

Exercise 7

Exercise 8

Exercise 9

Exercise 10

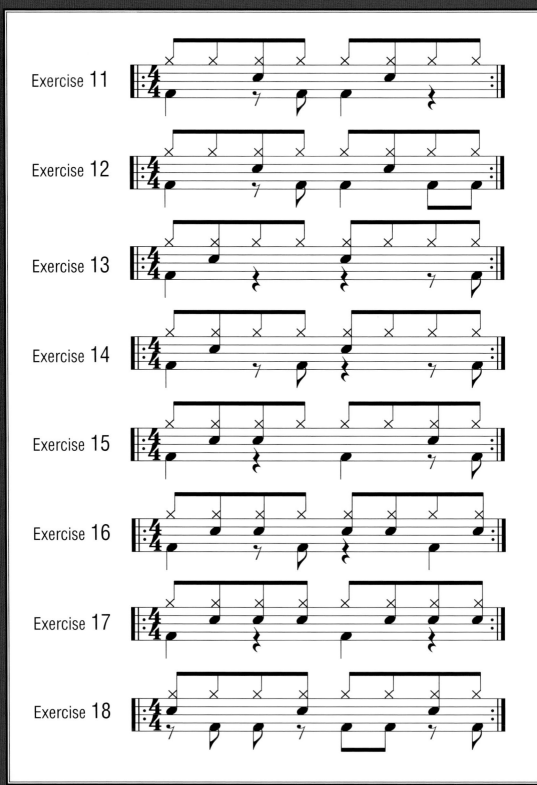

Exercise 11

Exercise 12

Exercise 13

Exercise 14

Exercise 15

Exercise 16

Exercise 17

Exercise 18

Exercise 19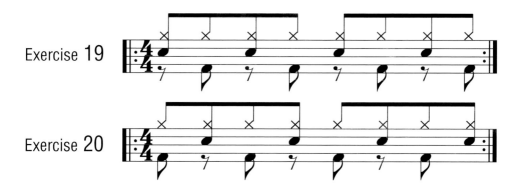

Exercise 20

DIFFERENT VOICES FOR ROCK BEATS

Now that you have learned some basic rock beats, there are many different ways you can apply them to the drums. Here are just a few of the ways that you can get a bit of variety from the basic rock beat pattern.

RIDE CYMBAL

The ride cymbal is used in much the same way as the hi-hats. It provides a continuous rhythm against which the snare and the bass drum create the beat. The ride cymbal's sound is much more open than the hi-hat, as each stroke rings out the note of the cymbal. For this reason, the ride is usually played during the louder feature parts of a song, such as during the chorus or solos.

All of the patterns you have played can also be played on the ride cymbal to create a different effect. As an exercise, practice changing from the hi-hat to the ride cymbal without stopping, like this:

Once you get the hang of it, try shortening the amount of time you spend on the ride and the hi-hat. Here it is with one bar on each:

You can try any variation on this exercise, right down to alternating between the hi-hat and the ride cymbal on each note. This can make for a really interesting beat! Try it first with the ride cymbal on the off beat:

Then give it a go with the ride on the beat:

FLOOR TOM

Another great variation for the 8th note rock beat is to apply the hi-hat pattern to the toms. This sort of beat is used a lot in popular music to give a deep, pounding beat.

SNARE DRUM

All of the alternate patterns you have looked at so far concentrate on changing the location of the 8th note hi-hat, but here is an example of how you can get a different sound from the snare drum:

1 Lay the stick down on the snare with the butt about 4 inches in from the hi-hat side of the snare rim. Hold the stick so that the end of it sticks out of the rim on the other side at about 2 o'clock.

2 While keeping the palm of your hand and the butt of the stick on the snare head, bend your hand at the wrist and lift the stick up and then back down on the rim. This will produce a 'choc' sound. Try it with more and then less of the stick protruding over the edge of the drum. There is a sweet spot where it will make a very pleasing, solid sound. This is called a snare 'click' or 'choc' and is commonly used in quieter songs as an alternative to hitting the snare.

Try applying all of these variations to the rock beats that you have already learned. Each one of them adds more vocabulary to what you can 'say' on the drums.

At the end of the book there are some more complex variations on the basic rock beat that you can try if you are feeling confident and up for a challenge.

ANATOMY OF A SONG

While each song that you listen to in your music collection or on the radio is different in many ways, most popular music shares a common structure that basically makes the foundation of a song the same. Songs are made up of fundamental sections that help tell a story or move the listener through a journey. The basic sections of a song are:

- ## INTRODUCTION
  The introduction is generally an element of the main melody of the song played at the beginning.

- ## VERSE
  The verses of a song tell the story. While they often follow the same melody each time, the words of the verse will change.

- ## CHORUS
  The chorus is different, both rhythmically and melodically, to the verses, and the lyrics of the chorus will repeat throughout the song. Choruses tend to be larger sounding and more complex.

- ## BRIDGE
  The bridge is a musical transition that connects two parts of a song. If you hear a section of a song that is melodically or vocally different to the verses and the chorus, most of the time it is the bridge.

The way that you play the drums will depend on which part of the song you are playing.

In the verses, the vocals are usually the feature, so quiet or controlled sounds are most appropriate. You don't want to overpower the melody or lyrics. The hi-hat is commonly used in verses because it is quieter and more precise than the ride cymbal, which continues to shimmer or ring when you aren't playing it.

The chorus demands a bigger sound, as does the bridge. The ride cymbal is more frequently used in these sections, along with a heavier hand on the snare drum.

Listen to some of your favorite songs and pick where the verse, chorus and bridge start and end, then see if you can hear what the drums are doing differently in each section.

PLAYING ALONG WITH A RECORDING

One of the best ways to practice and get a feel for how a song moves from one section to the next is to play along with one.

Whether you are playing to a song on the radio or to a track from your favorite CD, playing along with a recording is loads of fun and helps you in the following ways:

- ## UNDERSTANDING THE FLOW OF THE SONG
  Listening and feeling a song change while you are playing is a great way to naturally learn the changes that occur and how they affect your playing.

- ## LISTENING
  You must listen very carefully to the music to play along with a recording, while at the same time concentrating on playing a beat. This sort of concentrated listening is difficult at first, but it is exactly the sort of thing you do whenever you play with a band. Listening to the other instruments and to the sound that you are creating as a whole is the basis of great music.

- ## TIMING
  Like playing with a metronome, playing along with a recording will train you to keep good time. You can only learn how to do something by doing it, and you can only learn to do something well by doing it a lot. Most music is recorded with very solid time, so playing along with a recording is a great way to practice playing in time.

Before you start playing along with all of your favorite songs, make sure that you are very comfortable playing at least one rock beat. If you can't play a beat for a couple of minutes without making a mistake, you will find it tough to play it along with a recording.

When you choose the first song to play with, start with something at a medium or slower tempo. You want to be able to concentrate on staying in time and listening while you are playing, and you don't need to be worrying about breakneck speeds on top of that.

It is very important that you can hear the music clearly. If you are playing on practice pads, this should be fairly straightforward, but if you are playing on a drum kit and have to worry about deafening the neighbors and yourself, it can be more complicated.

The best trick I have found for getting the right mix of music and drums is pretty simple: get a pair of in-ear headphones to listen to the music and buy some cheap industrial headphones from a hardware store. The headphones protect your ears from a battering and make it much easier to hear the music and the drums clearly at similar levels.

When you first try to play along with a recording, start with just one of the elements of the rock beat, like you did at the start of the rock beats section. This example uses the hi-hat:

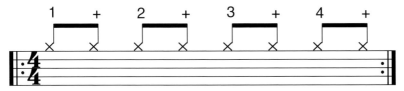

First find the beat in the song and count along with it. This is something you can practice whenever you listen to music. If you have any difficulty finding the beat, listen for the snare; remember, it will be on 2 and 4. Finding the first beat of the bar is easier if you remember that a new part of the song (verse, chorus or bridge) will almost always start on 1.

Once you are comfortable counting quarter notes (1, 2, 3, 4) and 8th notes (1 + 2 + 3 + 4 +) over the top of the song, start playing the 8th note hi-hat pattern along with it. It is really important that you don't rush this; play only the hi-hat pattern with the song for a few minutes. Make sure that you stay in time with the song the whole time. Once you feel comfortable playing the hi-hat along with the music, try playing just the snare and bass drum parts with no hi-hat.

Can you hear the beat come together with the music? Once you feel comfortable that you are in time, try putting all of the parts together with the music. It can help to start with just the hi-hat for a few bars so you get the time right.

If you don't have anyone else to play with, playing with a recording is the next best thing. It helps your timing, hones your listening, practices your beats and exposes you to all sorts of new ideas as you listen to what other drummers are playing in the songs.

FILLS

You have already seen some of the ways to change the beat to fulfil the needs of different parts of the song, but how can you tie all of these different beats together to make a song?

Drum fills are short patterns used to bridge the gaps between sections of a song, such as the verse and the chorus. A fill can be as small as the crash of a cymbal or as large as your imagination, and the song, will allow. In this section, you will learn how to construct a fill and try some different types. Here is where those rudiments really come in handy, so I hope you have been practicing!

The simplest type of fill simply acts as a way of marking a change in a song or changing your beat from the hi-hat to the ride cymbal. This is most often used when moving from the verse of a song to the chorus. In this example, you play a crash cymbal on beat 1 of the bar before moving to the ride cymbal.

Many fills end with the crash cymbal, as it is a great way to punctuate a change in the music. Keeping the crash on 1, here are a few variations that use the snare and the toms:

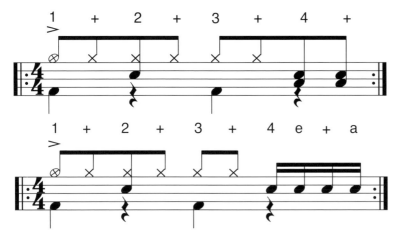

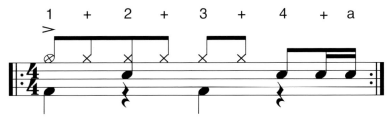

You can also try these three examples around the kit for a different sound. Here are some variations to get your creativity going:

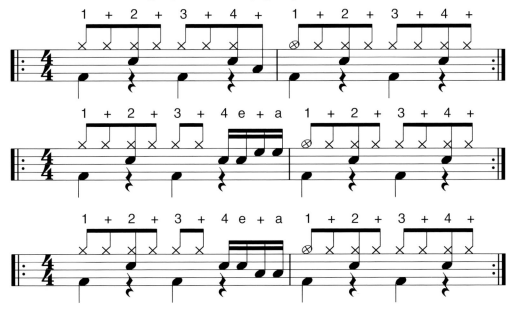

It is important to find the best sticking combinations for a fill. Otherwise you can find yourself wildly reaching across the kit because the last stroke of the fill is played by the same hand that is supposed to play the first note of your beat. Remember, the best hand to play the crash at the beginning of the second bar is the same hand that you use for the hi-hat. For instance, if you are right-handed, try to end the fill on your left hand to give the right one a chance to get back to the cymbal, and vice versa for left-handed drummers.

The correct sticking is really important for this fill, as your hands need to get around the kit really fast.

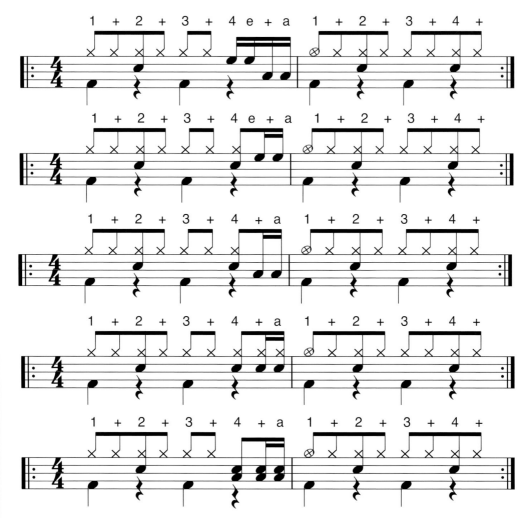

As you can see, there are plenty of variations that can be applied to just a couple of simple patterns.

FLAMS

The flam is a straightforward rudiment that offers a new type of sound to your vocabulary on the drums. It is particularly suited to fills. A flam consists of two strokes played very close together: one soft and the other accented. The sound produced is very much like the word flam: 'fl-am'. A flam is written like this:

The quieter leading note in a flam is called a grace note. To play a flam, start with your sticks at different heights above the drum. The stick playing the grace note should be just above the drum (about 2 inches) and the other stick should start from higher up (about 8 inches).

Bring the sticks down on the drum at the same speed so the stick that begins its journey closer to the drum will hit first: this is the grace note. The sticks should come down close enough to each other that it produces almost one sound, but not so close that they hit the drum at the same time.

Make sure when you are practicing flams that you alternate the grace note hand each time, so that you can play a flam starting with both your right and left hands. This is a good example of the earlier lesson about consistent strokes – the smaller the stroke (i.e. the closer the stick is to the drum when you begin a stroke), the quieter it will be. If your sticks are only 2 inches from the drum head, it doesn't matter how hard you try to hit the drum, it isn't going to be loud. This is useful to remember when you want to play quietly or if you want to control one stroke in comparison to another, such as in flams or paradiddles.

Here are some fills that include flams. For each of these examples, begin with the fill and then play into a simple rock beat.

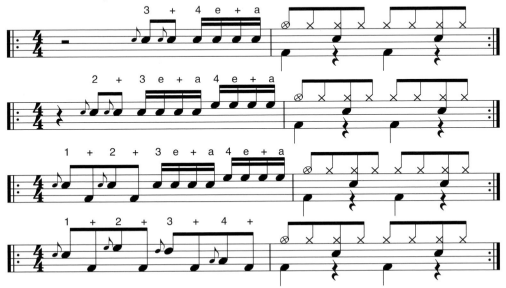

These flam fills are longer than the first group and are geared more toward being played at the start of a drum beat rather than during a song. There are also plenty of ways that flams can be used inside a beat as well.

The two most important things to remember when developing your repertoire of fills are to listen to other drummers and to experiment. Try as many different combinations that you can think of, and when you are at a loss, listen to other drummers and copy what they are playing. There is an endless supply of ideas out there!

ADVANCED EXERCISES

O nce you feel confident with all of the exercises, here are a couple of variations that you can apply to them which are a little more complex and rewarding.

OPEN HI-HAT

Up until now, all the rock beat exercises have been played on a closed hi-hat, but, as you are well aware, the hi-hat also works in the open position.

WASHY HI-HAT

Some types of music, particularly heavier rock and metal, call for a 'washy' sound on the hi-hats. You can get this by lifting your hi-hat foot slightly so that the top and bottom cymbals are only just touching. When you hit the hi-hat, you will get a sound that is closer to a crash cymbal.

Make sure that the two hi-hat cymbals are still in contact with each other. If you lift your foot too high off the pedal and they aren't touching, you will only be hitting the top cymbal and the effect will be lost.

CONTROLLED OPEN HI-HAT

The hi-hat can also be opened in shorter, controlled bursts to create extra color to your beats. To get a good, controlled open hi-hat sound, start with the cymbals closed tight. At the same time as the stick hits the top cymbal, open the hi-hats slightly. Once you get an even, sizzle sound from the hi-hat, try closing it off again with your foot.

This can be applied to your rock beat hi-hat patterns in all sorts of ways. Here are some examples of different hi-hat patterns that you can try over the rock beats you have already learned.

The notes that are joined together by an arch are 'tied'. Think of the arch as the open sizzle sound, starting on the stroke where the arch begins and ending with a closed foot and another stoke where the arch ends. In this exercise, the hi-hat opens on the + of 4 and closes again on 1.

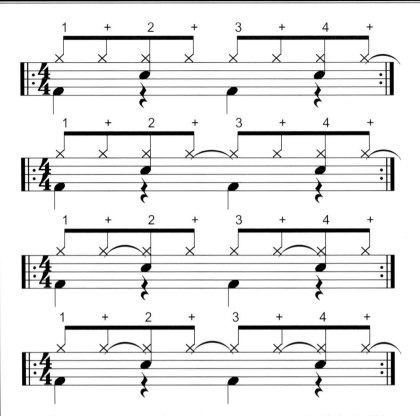

This final exercise has the hi-hat opening on all of the 'off beats' (+). This combination is very popular in dance music.

HI-HAT VARIATIONS

The following exercises show you some other hi-hat patterns that you can try instead of the simple 8th note pattern used thus far in this book. Each one of these patterns should be played over all of the bass drum variations on pages 38–42.

THE 16TH NOTE HI-HAT PATTERN

Playing 16th notes on the hi-hat is another variation that is really useful.

This pattern can be played either one- or two-handed. Playing 16th notes on the hi-hat with one hand is similar an 8th note rock beat; there are just more notes.

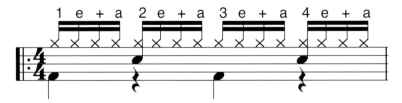

You can also play 16th notes with two hands, each playing single stroke on the hi-hat like this:

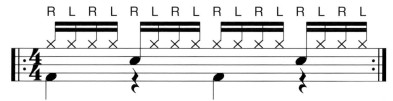

You will notice that each of the different ways of playing the 16th note hi-hat pattern (with one or two hands) sound different. When playing this beat, try both ways and see which is more suited to the music you are playing.

Here is another variation on the 16th note hi-hat pattern:

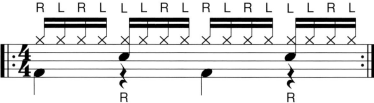

In this pattern, note the sticking. In the first two-handed 16th note pattern, the hi-hat is played on every 16th note except for 2 and 4, where the right hand is playing the snare. In this pattern, the left hand plays 3 stokes in a row to make up for the right hand's absence. This can be a difficult pattern to get used to, so take it slowly and just practice the hands before you try playing any of the bass drum combinations along with it.

16TH NOTE HI-HAT VARIATIONS

Here are two more one-handed patterns for the hi-hat that also include different combinations of 16th notes. All of these patterns can be applied to the bass drum variations earlier in the book.

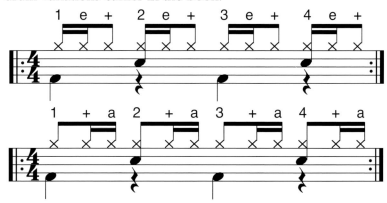

HI-HAT FOOT

Now for some genuine four-way independence exercises. Up until now, you have completed multiple patterns using three different limbs. Now you will add the fourth: your hi-hat foot. The following exercises apply simple patterns that should be played with the hi-hat foot in the same way that you would play the bass drum. To ensure a clear 'chick' sound from the hi-hat, you should play the hand pattern on the ride cymbal.

Apply the following hi-hat foot patterns to the beats you have learned so far.

HI-HAT 2 AND 4

This pattern has the hi-hat foot playing along with the snare on 2 and 4. If you start by applying this to the first rock beat that you learned with the bass drum on 1 and 3, you will see that your feet are alternating, as though you are walking. You can talk and write and eat while you are walking, so by now you should be able to play a simple rock beat while you do it as well.

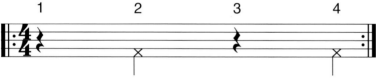

HI-HAT ALL 4

This pattern is starting to get you to the point of playing the hi-hat foot in a beat. This constant quarter note pattern is quiet compared to the rest of the parts of your drum beat. However, it adds a subtle but important emphasis on 1, 2, 3 and 4, which, as you will remember from the start of the book, is where the beat is in 4/4 music. That is where the groove is.

CONCLUSION

One thing I have discovered after years of playing drums and seeing bands of all different types is that drummers are a very giving community of musicians. It is rare to find a drummer who doesn't want to talk about their drums, the sort of music they are playing, who they are listening to, what they have just learned or what they are hoping to learn next. Make use of this whenever you can: speak to other drummers, learn about their experiences and tell them about your own.

There are no secrets in music. Teaching someone else how to play doesn't make you any less of a drummer and, because every individual who plays the instrument approaches it in a different way, the more people who are playing and sharing their knowledge, the more new ideas come to life.

Listen to new music. Listen to old music. No musician ever lost out from hearing something new or different, or from trying to play something they haven't tried before. You may not love every style of music you hear, but they all have something that is unique which adds to your musical vocabulary.

Finally, get drum lessons. You never stop learning. I have been to countless teachers in my time and every one of them has enriched my experiences on the drums and made me a better player much quicker than I ever could have become on my own.

ABOUT THE AUTHOR

Cameron Skews has been playing drums for 20 years in bands across a diverse range of musical styles, ranging from rock and funk to Irish, African and jazz. Whether playing the drums or teaching students aged from 3 to 60, Cameron is a passionate advocate for the drums and their impact.